ZEBRAS

Please visit our web site at: **www.garethstevens.com**
For a free color catalog describing Gareth Stevens Publishing's
list of high-quality books and multimedia programs, call
1-800-542-2595 (USA) or 1-800-387-3178 (Canada).
Gareth Stevens Publishing's fax: (414) 332-3567.

Library of Congress Cataloging-in-Publication Data

All about zebras.
   Zebras.
      p. cm. — (All about wild animals)
      Previously published in Great Britain as: All about zebras. 2002.
      ISBN 0-8368-4190-5 (lib. bdg.)
      1. Zebras—Juvenile literature. I. Title. II. Series.
   QL795.Z42A58   2004
   599.665'7—dc22
                                           2004041633

This edition first published in 2005 by
Gareth Stevens Publishing
A World Almanac Education Group Company
330 West Olive Street, Suite 100
Milwaukee, Wisconsin 53212 USA

This U.S. edition copyright © 2005 by Gareth Stevens, Inc. Original edition
copyright © 2002 by DeAgostini UK Limited. First published in 2002 as
My Animal Kingdom: All About Zebras by DeAgostini UK Ltd., Griffin House,
161 Hammersmith Road, London W6 8SD, England. Additional end matter
copyright © 2005 by Gareth Stevens, Inc.

Editorial and design: Tucker Slingsby Ltd., London
Gareth Stevens series editor: Catherine Gardner
Gareth Stevens art direction: Tammy West

Picture Credits
NHPA — John Shaw: 6, 12, 13; Nigel J. Dennis: 7; Christophe Ratier: 10,
    15; Stephen Krasemann: 11; Steve Robinson: 14; Jonathan and Angela
    Scott: 17, 19, 22; Martin Harvey: 17, 27; Daryl Balfour: 18–19; Daniel
    Heuclin: 27.
Oxford Scientific Films — Daniel J. Cox: front cover and title page; David
    Cayless: 8; Steve Turner: 9, 13; Rafi Ben-Shahar: 11; Richard Packwood:
    15; Chris Knights: 16; Andrew Park: 20; Tim Jackson: 21; Des and
    Jen Bartlett: 23, 29; Rob Nunnington: 24–25; Mike Hill: 28; William
    Paton: 26.

Printed in the United States of America

1 2 3 4 5 6 7 8 9 08 07 06 05 04

ALL about WILD ANIMALS

ZEBRAS

Gareth Stevens Publishing
A WORLD ALMANAC EDUCATION GROUP COMPANY

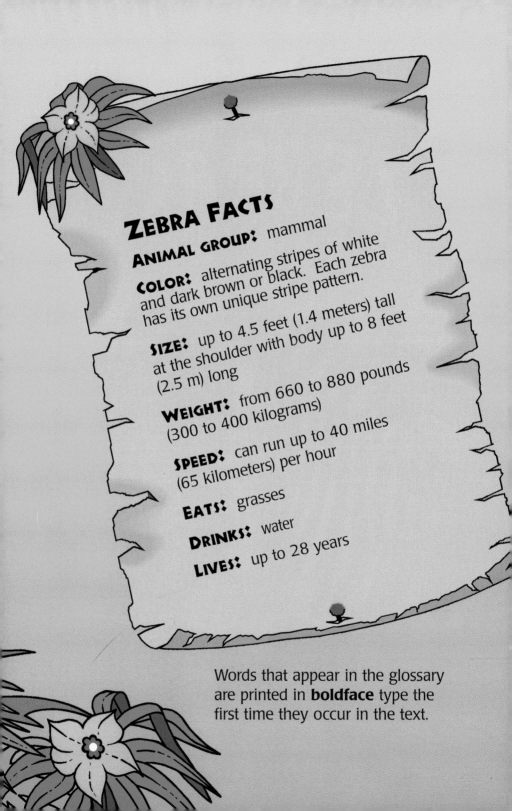

Zebra Facts

Animal group: mammal

Color: alternating stripes of white and dark brown or black. Each zebra has its own unique stripe pattern.

Size: up to 4.5 feet (1.4 meters) tall at the shoulder with body up to 8 feet (2.5 m) long

Weight: from 660 to 880 pounds (300 to 400 kilograms)

Speed: can run up to 40 miles (65 kilometers) per hour

Eats: grasses

Drinks: water

Lives: up to 28 years

Words that appear in the glossary are printed in **boldface** type the first time they occur in the text.

CONTENTS

A Closer Look

Under their striped coats, zebras look a lot like **domestic** horses. Like domestic horses, zebras have sturdy bodies that are shaped like barrels. Zebras are covered with short hair, and they have short manes on their necks. Zebras, like horses, have strong legs, which are built for running away from **predators** — or kicking any enemies that get too close. Their hooved feet help them speed across the grasslands, or savannas, of Africa.

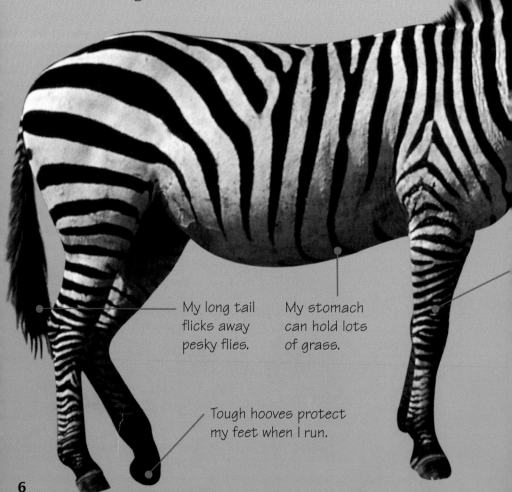

My long tail flicks away pesky flies.

My stomach can hold lots of grass.

Tough hooves protect my feet when I run.

- No two zebras have the same pattern of stripes.

- Zebras probably recognize each other by their patterns. After a zebra is born, the mother and **foal** learn each other's pattern.

- The zebra's stripes help break up the outline of its body, so it is hard for a predator to focus on any one zebra in the herd.

My striped mane stands upright.

My eyes are spaced far apart to help me spot danger from all directions.

I have strong legs to help me run long distances.

Zebras have large, upright ears, which they can move around to pick up sounds from all directions. Their eyes are big and set on either side of their heads, so they can see all around, too. A zebra's strong senses of hearing, sight, and smell help it detect danger in enough time to run away from its enemies.

HARD HOOVES

A zebra walks on the tips of its toes. Each foot has only one large middle toe, which is protected by a thick, hard hoof. A zebra's hoof is like a human's toenail, but it wraps around the zebra's whole toe. Hooves are made out of keratin, just like a human's toenails, and they do not wear out. Like a person's toenails, a zebra's hooves keep growing throughout its life.

TOUGH TEETH

A zebra's teeth are made for chewing grass. It has front teeth, or incisors, that are like pincers. The zebra uses them to nip off grass stems. Then it uses its flat cheek teeth to grind the stems. The grinding action wears down the zebra's teeth, but worn-out teeth are not a problem for a zebra. Its cheek teeth keep growing all its life.

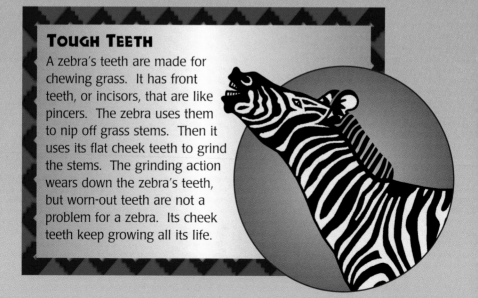

My large ears
turn to pick
up even very
soft sounds.

My eyes are on
the sides of my
head. They give
me a view to the
back and sides
of my body, not
just the front.

I have a keen
nose. I can
sniff out my
friends and
my enemies.

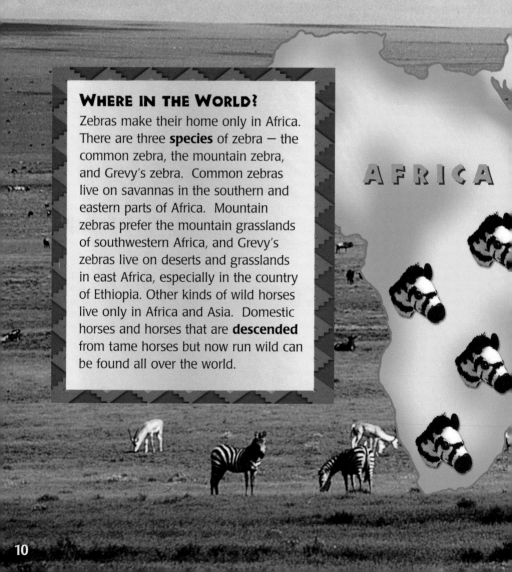

HOME, SWEET HOME

Common zebras, which are also known as plains zebras, live on the savannas of Africa. Savannas have hot, dry weather, especially during summer. Zebras need to get a big drink of water at least once a day, so they do not wander too far from rivers or **water holes**.

WHERE IN THE WORLD?

Zebras make their home only in Africa. There are three **species** of zebra — the common zebra, the mountain zebra, and Grevy's zebra. Common zebras live on savannas in the southern and eastern parts of Africa. Mountain zebras prefer the mountain grasslands of southwestern Africa, and Grevy's zebras live on deserts and grasslands in east Africa, especially in the country of Ethiopia. Other kinds of wild horses live only in Africa and Asia. Domestic horses and horses that are **descended** from tame horses but now run wild can be found all over the world.

AFRICA

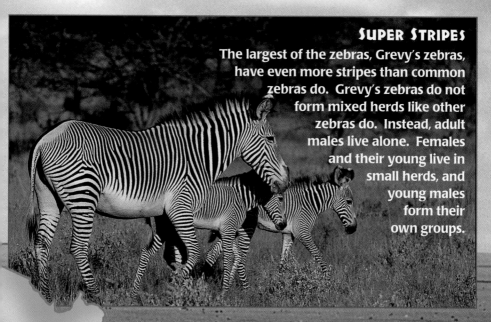

SUPER STRIPES

The largest of the zebras, Grevy's zebras, have even more stripes than common zebras do. Grevy's zebras do not form mixed herds like other zebras do. Instead, adult males live alone. Females and their young live in small herds, and young males form their own groups.

MEETING PLACE

Zebras often drink water at dawn and dusk. They meet other **grazing** animals at a water hole. All the animals keep watch for predators and warn each other if enemies threaten. The more eyes there are, the better!

NEIGHBORS

Savannas are home to more than three hundred thousand common zebras. They share the grassy savannas with lots of other plant-eating animals. Not all the animals eat the same plants, so there is enough food for them all. Many grazing animals move from place to place, which allows grass to grow back in one area while they eat in another.

HARD HORNS

An oryx is not a fussy feeder. It can chew up coarse grass and even eat thorny shrubs. Like other types of **antelopes**, an oryx can speed away when enemies are near. It can wound a predator with its long, spearlike horns, which can be up to 3 feet (1 meter) long!

Tough Ox

Hartebeests often graze with zebras, wildebeests and gazelles. A hartebeest is a type of antelope that enjoys nibbling juicy, young grasses. It also chews dry grasses that other grazers do not want. A hartebeest can run for hours without resting. Its name fits. *Hartebeest* means "tough ox."

Bird Watchers

Zebras and other animals often graze near ostriches. At over 6 feet (2 m) tall, ostriches are great lookouts. With their huge eyes, ostriches spot predators from a long distance. Then they hiss a warning.

THE FAMILY

Common zebras live in family herds that include up to six females and their young. The herd has one adult male, or stallion. He protects the herd. Sometimes several family herds join together to form a big herd on the **plain**. Even in a crowd, zebras can recognize other family members by the patterns of their stripes and their sounds and smells.

Zebras usually have their young in spring. A newborn foal has a short body, long legs, and a longer and furrier striped coat than an adult zebra. It is about 3 feet (1 m) tall and weighs about 65 pounds (30 kilograms), which is about the weight of a seven-year-old child. The mother zebra stays close to her newborn. She does not let other females, called mares, get close, probably so her foal has time to learn her stripe pattern first.

WOBBLY WALKING

A newborn zebra does not have time to lie around. It takes its first wobbly steps within an hour after it is born. When it is only a few hours old, it can run with its mother and her herd.

BABY FILE

BIRTH

A female zebra usually has one foal a year. A mare cares for her foal and keeps it safe from lions and other kinds of predators. At first, the foal does not eat grass, but it drinks its mother's milk.

THREE MONTHS

The foal grows fast. It still drinks its mother's milk, but by the time it is three months old, it eats grass, too. While the foal grazes with its herd, it remains close to its mother until her next foal is born.

ONE TO TWO YEARS

When the foal is two years old, it can take care of itself. Young males leave their herds and form their own groups. Some of the mares also leave to start herds with young stallions.

MUD BATH

A zebra does not keep clean by washing with water. Instead, it rolls in mud or dust. When the mud dries, the zebra shakes its body, and the mud — along with loose hair and dry skin — falls off. Rolling in the dust gets rid of nasty, biting bugs, too. Sometimes, zebras help **groom** each other, but rolling in the dust seems to be much more fun!

17

LIFE WITH THE HERD

On African savannas, it does not rain much during the dry season. Many water holes dry up. The grass turns yellow and dies. Food becomes **scarce**, and common zebras may need to travel long distances to find new feeding grounds. If they stayed in one place, they would starve. Antelopes and wildebeests join the zebras in their search for food.

Zebras make many different sounds, and each sound has a different meaning. A zebra mother gives a high-pitched whinny to keep in touch with her foal. Zebras that spot danger snicker or neigh to warn the others. A stallion's alarm call is a yelping bark.

REAR GUARD

Even when zebras travel with other animals, they stay together in their family herds. A herd walks in a line with the chief mare and her foal at the front. The stallion stays at the back of the line as a guard.

WILD WATERS

Zebras may travel a long distance to find food during the dry season. They sometimes cross rivers where crafty crocodiles lie in wait. To go across, the zebras jump into the water and swim as fast as they can to the other side. Most of the zebras cross safely, but if it can, a hungry crocodile grabs a zebra by the leg and pulls it underwater to drown it.

Favorite Foods

Like domestic horses, zebras mainly eat grass. They graze on all kinds of grass, from tender, green **shoots** to tough, dry stalks. Grass has few **nutrients**, so zebras have to eat a lot of it to stay healthy. They spend up to sixteen hours a day eating!

GRASS GUZZLERS

Zebras like to nibble fresh grass shoots, but they usually have to make do with old, tough stalks. When grass is scarce, zebras look for leaves, fruit, and shoots of other plants. They nip off the food with their front teeth and then grind it to a pulp with their cheek teeth.

GRAZERS AND BROWSERS

More than forty kinds of plant-eating animals live on the African savannas. They all eat different parts of various plants, so there is enough food to go around. Grazing animals, including zebras, gazelles, and buffaloes, eat different parts or growth stages of grasses. Browsing animals, such as giraffes, nibble shrubs and bushes or pull juicy leaves from trees.

DANGER!

The animals of the African savannas are divided into two groups — the hunters and the hunted. Zebras are hunted! A zebra makes a tasty meal that feeds a whole **pride** of lions, so zebras must watch for predators day and night. Living in herds helps keep zebras safe. Many pairs of eyes keeping watch for hungry predators are better than just one pair.

BEWARE! LIONS!

The lion is one of the zebra's most dangerous enemies. Lions are clever **carnivores** that hunt in groups. Female lions stalk their prey at dusk. When they find a herd of zebras, they try to creep as close as possible and surround the herd. Usually, they single out one particular zebra and attack it together.

ON GUARD

Zebras have lots of tricks to escape from predators. They can run fast, and they can kick very hard. Their stripes help, too. It is tough for a predator to pick out a single zebra from a herd of stripes!

FOOD CHAINS

Savanna plants and animals depend on each other for food. Plants and animals linked together by food make up a food chain. Grass, zebras, and leopards are in a food chain. Zebras eat grass, and then leopards eat the zebras.

A Zebra's Day

6:00 AM The Sun began to rise. My herd had moved during the night, and I had managed to find a patch of very tasty grass. I munched slowly, watching for any enemies.

8:00 AM We met giraffes and wildebeests at the water hole. We drank with them. Then we all walked off together to eat. It is safer to be in a big group.

12 NOON It was hot. We moved into the shade of a few trees to keep cool. I flicked away flies with my tail. The foals settled down to sleep.

2:00 PM I felt quite sleepy, so I dozed off, too. There were some ostriches nearby, and I knew they would warn us if any predators approached.

5:00 PM It was cooler, and the young foals played while we watched for danger.

 6:00 PM As the Sun began to set in the sky, we made our way to the river to get a long, cool drink.

 8:00 PM My herd was grazing peacefully when I suddenly heard a soft sound in the undergrowth — lions! I snorted and barked to warn the others, and we raced away.

 9:00 PM Safe again. Three lionesses tried to attack us, but they gave up the chase. I stayed at the back of the herd as we ran, ready to kick any lionesses who got too close.

 12:00 MIDNIGHT We found some nice, juicy grass and settled down to eat. We need to stay strong and healthy! I heard a leopard in the distance, but it did not come near us.

 4:00 AM We had a peaceful night of grazing and dozing. It will be daylight soon. I think I'll just take a few more bites of grass to keep me going!

25

RELATIVES

Zebras are part of a group of animals in the horse family. Ten thousand years ago, there were many different types of wild horses living all over the world. Today, the wild members of the horse family are found only in parts of Asia and Africa. The domestic members of the family live all around the world.

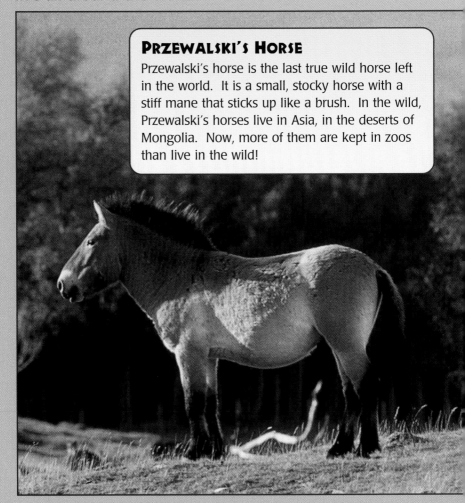

PRZEWALSKI'S HORSE

Przewalski's horse is the last true wild horse left in the world. It is a small, stocky horse with a stiff mane that sticks up like a brush. In the wild, Przewalski's horses live in Asia, in the deserts of Mongolia. Now, more of them are kept in zoos than live in the wild!

ANCIENT TAPIR

Tapirs, which live in the Asian and South American rain forests, are distant relatives of zebras. While a tapir has a lot in common with the horse family, it looks like a hairy pig with a short trunk — a look that did not change much in its 35-million-year history!

DID YOU KNOW?

- The horse family belongs to a group of animals called perissodactyls. They are hooved animals that have an odd number of toes. This group includes horses, tapirs, and rhinoceroses.

- One of the first horses, *Eohippus*, lived more than 50 million years ago. It was only the size of a greyhound dog.

HUNGRY ONAGER

Another Asian member of the horse family is the onager. Onagers live in groups, each led by a chief male. Like a zebra, an onager eats grass, from juicy, new shoots to tough, dry stems. In summer, onagers feed high up on hillsides. In winter, the herds move to warmer valleys.

Humans and Zebras

For many years, zebras have been worth more to humans dead than alive. People hunt zebras for meat and also for their unusual and valuable striped coats. People kill zebras because they think zebras take too much grazing land and water away from their domestic animals. On the other hand, people prize the horse, a relative of the zebra, because they can tame and train it.

Horse Racing

Wild horses were tamed about sixty-five hundred years ago. Since then, people have trained horses to do many different jobs and play some sports. Horses star in sports such as show jumping, polo, and racing. Winning horses can earn lots of money for their owners.

ZOO ZEBRAS

Zebras are in danger. Only about fifteen hundred Grevy's zebras are left in the wild, and mountain zebras also are threatened. There are more common zebras, but most of them must be in protected places where hunting is not allowed. Zebras are popular animals in zoos all over the world and on **safaris** in Africa. People like to look at these stripy animals.

- Two kinds of zebra have died out during the past 150 years.

- In Ancient Rome, zebras were called horse tigers and were used as circus animals.

- Domestic horses are measured in hands. One hand equals 4 inches (10 centimeters). Zebras are about 14 hands high.

Glossary

ANTELOPES
Animals that look like deer but have long horns without any branches. They live in Africa and parts of Asia and are known for their fast running speed.

CARNIVORES
Animals that eat meat.

DESCENDED
Came from a particular ancestor; from the same family as another but living at a later time.

DOMESTIC
No longer wild; trained or tamed to live with people.

FOAL
A young animal of the horse family.

GRAZING
Feeding on growing plants.

GROOM
To clean and make neat, especially hair or fur.

NUTRIENTS
The parts of food needed by humans, animals, and plants to stay healthy.

PLAIN
A large, wide area of flat land.

PREDATORS
Animals that hunt other animals for food.

PRIDE
A group of lions that includes a few males, many females, and their cubs.

SAFARIS
Trips, often in Africa, to see, photograph, or hunt wild animals.

SCARCE
Rare and hard to find.

SHOOTS
Young plants that have just grown above the soil or new parts beginning to develop on a plant.

SPECIES
Groups of animals that have the same features, behaviors, and name.

WATER HOLES
Natural holes or low-lying areas that hold water.

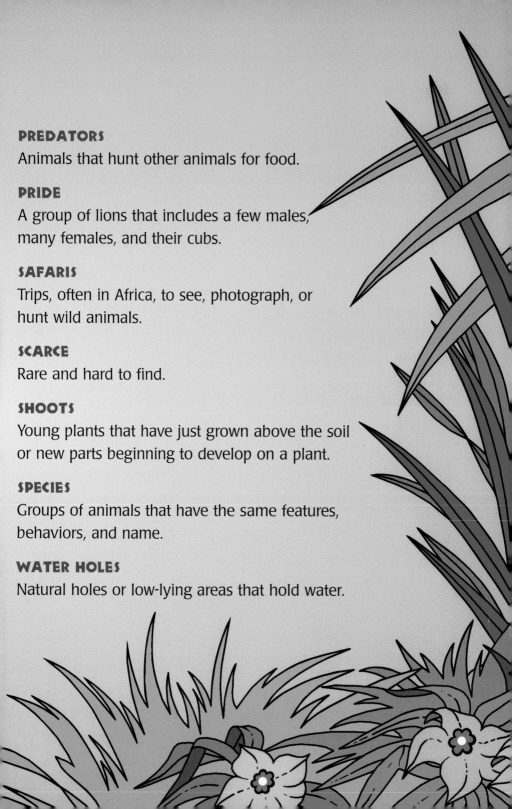

Index